KALE

Christopher Trotter

Photography by Caroline Trotter

*For Henry and his lovely bride Siobhan,
lots of love*

© Christopher Trotter 2015

Published by Momentum publishing.

A CIP catalogue record for this book is available from the British Library.

ISBN 978-0-9926830-3-0

Produced by Print & Design, University of St Andrews
Website: www.st-andrews.ac.uk/printanddesign

Printed by Latimer Trend & Company Limited

Distributed by Christopher Trotter
Tel: 07739049639

CONTENTS

INTRODUCTION

Kale is for me a particularly important vegetable. It has strong connotations in the Scots diet and with Scottish history in general. The "Kailyard" or kitchen garden was as important to the Scot as the potato plot was to the Irish peasant. And the word kail became synonymous with eating. Kail was the word used for the midday meal; mothers would call their "bairns", "Come in for your kail", whether it was indeed the green vegetable or some other simple meal. The kail bells would chime at 2 o'clock in Edinburgh to announce dinner time. Kale is THE Scottish vegetable.

It is also synonymous with Scotland because it can survive a harsh Scottish winter and I can wander into my snow-clad garden and the only thing visible is the tops of the vibrant green leaves thrusting through the icy carpet. Indeed, like the brussels sprout, the flavour changes from a mild to a more spicy flavour after it has been frosted, when some of the starch has been converted to sugar. The deeply intense flavours marry well with spices, nuts and fruit.

VARIETIES

There are many more names for kale than there are actual varieties, as some have as many as four different names depending where you come from! Kale is a borecole and is part of the species "Brassica Oleracea", a cabbage whose central leaves do not form a head like a wild cabbage.

CURLY is perhaps the most common and is the one most people associate with the word kale. Curly has loosely crinkled green or purple leaves. It's also known as Collard greens in America. The younger leaves are good raw in salads and smoothies. It has a fibrous stalk and a peppery, bitter flavour the older it gets.

BLACK or CAVOLO NERO, sometimes also known as Lacianto or Dinosaur, has long dark blue/ green leaves with a deep earthy flavour; not so bitter perhaps as curly but nutty.

RED RUSSIAN or RAGGED JACK has flat-fringed leaves with reddish edges and beautiful red-purple stems which, although they can be fibrous, are colourful if finely chopped in a dish.

REDBOR or RED is a very pretty purple with crinkly leaves but is not common and has little flavour.

ASPARAGUS is flat-leaved with pale green leaves with a pinkish tinge; its thin stalks and more delicate flavour make it ideal for salads and quick cooking.

Then there is SEA kale, which is also a brassica, but called "Crambe Maritima", and grows wild around British coasts. It is also farmed and makes an early-in-the-year substitute for asparagus.

NUTRITION

Kale is often termed a "super food" and the nutritionists get very excited about it as the great new food. However, it has been around a long time and I am delighted that its reputation has improved from being mere animal feed! It has powerful antioxidants such as cartenoids and flavonoids which help prevent various cancers. It is low on calories and high in fibre with no fat. It aids digestion and intestinal cleansing. It is high in iron, in fact per 100g it has more than beef! Iron is good for proper liver function. It has more calcium per calorie than milk.

High in vitamin A, which is good for vision and skin; high in vitamin C which is good for the immune system, general metabolism and hydration. It also provides vitamin K which protects against cancers. 100g of kale provides all the betacarotene a women needs in a day. It is also a good source of lutein; one of the cartenoids that helps prevent the eye disease AMD or Age-Related Macular Degeneration, the most common cause of visual loss in the elderly.

BUYING AND STORING

Commercially, kale is traditionally grown from mid-May to July for winter use but growers are beginning to realise that it is being sought-after year round, and Pillars of Hercules in Fife is trying to meet that demand. Otherwise, look for Red Russian from October to April. Black kale from October to January and Curly, September to March. The shoots or "Dragon shoots" are available in the spring. Other names for it are "Thousand head" or "Hungry gap".

If bought on the stalk, it will keep in a cool place for a week but even the leaves stored in the fridge will keep for several days. Guy Watson, in the Riverford Farm Cook Book, gives a sense of the "robustness of flavour and texture" in order, from the strong down: Black, Curly, Redbor (red), Dragon shoots and Red Russian. In the recipes, I suggest different types for different recipes but really it's a matter of making use of what is available and choosing the recipe to suit! Please do use the stems where possible, even if it is only in a soup.

SEA KALE WITH BROWN BUTTER

Sea Kale grows wild along our coast but is a sadly neglected vegetable; its sweet flavour a true harbinger of spring. There is only one grower in Scotland – Sandy Pattullo in Glamis. Sea kale only takes minutes to cook and all you need is a pan of boiling, salted water.

INGREDIENTS

2 bunches Sea kale
200g butter
Juice of a lemon
Freshly ground black pepper
Hebridean salt

METHOD

1 Bring a large pot of salted water to the boil.
2 Plunge the Sea kale into the water and cook for about a minute. Lift out and drain on kitchen paper and then place on warm plates.
3 Put the butter in to a small pan or frying pan over a medium heat.
4 As the butter melts and heats, it will foam up and then die down and start to turn brown. Watch very carefully at this point and use your sense of smell. The butter should have a nutty smell and be golden brown. As soon as it is like this pour in the lemon juice. It will bubble up, and then pour the hot sauce through a sieve over the Sea kale tips.
5 A sprinkle of coarse Hebridean salt and black pepper is good.

SEA KALE WITH ORANGE HOLLANDAISE

This lovely, simple recipe comes from a chef and food writer I admire enormously, Rowley Leigh, who owns the Cafe des Anglais in London. I worked briefly with him when writing an article about him and found his approach to food and cooking inspiring.

INGREDIENTS

1kg Sea kale
250g unsalted butter
4 egg yolks
Juice of 2 blood oranges
Juice of half a lemon

METHOD

1   Make the hollandaise first by melting the butter in a pan, keep it warm but not too hot or the sauce will "split".
2   Using a stainless steel pan, whisk the yolks with the orange juice until it just thickens and goes slightly frothy. On no account allow it to get too thick.
3   Away from the heat, set the egg mixture pan on a damp cloth so that it doesn't move about, and slowly pour the melted butter on, whilst whisking the egg yolks vigorously. It will form a thick sauce. If it's too thick, add some of the milk residue from the melted butter and then a squeeze of lemon, and season with salt and pepper.
4   Cook the Sea kale as in the previous recipe.

THE BASIC RECIPE

Braised kale is a delicious dish on its own but is also the base for some of the recipes in the book and I refer to these in the ingredients as "base recipe".

I am not going to show quantities here as it's a matter of taste but once you have the idea, then you can experiment. All kales can be cooked in this manner; some take longer than others. Just remember: thick stalk slow; thin stalk quick!

Cooked in this manner, it is not necessary to separate the stalks from the leaves as the cooking time is long enough to soften them.

INGREDIENTS

Take several handfuls of kale and shred quite roughly
Cold-pressed rapeseed oil
A couple cloves of garlic, peeled and sliced thinly
Hebridean salt and coarse black pepper

METHOD

1   Plunge the kale into a pan of boiling, salted water.
2   Cook for about 3 minutes, depending on thickness of stalk.
3   Drain and refresh in cold water.
4   Drain and squeeze out as much water as possible.
5   Take a frying pan and add a little oil and stir in the garlic, then add the kale and mix through, season. Use straight away or set aside for recipes.

FOR A SIMPLE SUPPER DISH WITH BACON AND EGG:
Blanche the kale as above, then cook some strips of bacon in the pan before adding the garlic and kale, mix through and serve with a poached egg.

ROAST GARLIC SOUP WITH KALE AND GINGER

Based on an idea from the wonderful soup book by Bridgid Allen. You can use any kale here but the Curly does give a good colour. Cut the stalks separately from the fronds. Try using smoked garlic and not roasting it.

INGREDIENTS

2 onions peeled and sliced
Sunflower oil
300g kale
30g ginger root peeled and chopped
7 large cloves of garlic
2 potatoes peeled and chopped
1 tsp Chinese five spice
1 tsp Hebridean sea salt
Freshly ground black pepper
1.5 litres water

METHOD

1　Cook the onions gently in a large pot with a little oil, to soften.
2　Add the chopped kale stalks and the ginger and continue to cook gently for 10 minutes.
3　Meanwhile roast the garlic in a hot oven with a little oil for 10 minutes.
4　Stir in the chopped potatoes, the garlic, five spice, salt and black pepper and add the water.
5　Bring to the boil and add the kale fronds. Simmer gently for about 20 minutes and allow to cool a little before liquidising.

A swirl of sesame oil on top is delicious.

KALE AND BARLEY BROTH

Pork and ham go very well with kale and this is based on a recipe from F. Marion Macneill's book "The Scots kitchen". I use a strong pork stock or the left-over liquid from making brawn but you can equally well make it with a ham hock or stock remaining from a cooked ham and add bits of meat to it. A real winter warmer.

INGREDIENTS

100g barley soaked for a few hours in cold water
2 tblsp cold-pressed rapeseed oil
2 leeks, cut into small dice
200g kale with the stalks and fronds separated
1.5 litres good stock or water and a ham hock
Hebridean sea salt

METHOD

1   Cut the kale stalks into small pieces. This soup is not liquidised so you need to keep the pieces an even size.
2   Sweat the leek in the oil in a large pan and once softened add the chopped kale stalks. Stir to really mix through.
3   Drain and stir in the barley; discard the soaking water.
3   Add the stock, or water and ham, and bring to a boil.
4   Shred the kale fronds finely and add to the pan, with the salt.
5   Simmer gently until the barley is just cooked.

DRAGON SPROUTS WITH CHILLI AND RICE VINEGAR

These sprouts appear in the spring but you can also use purple sprouting. The name Dragon was given to me by Archie McDiarmid of Luvians Bottle shop who suggested a great wine to go with it – Leitz Dragonstone Riesling; brilliant wine and who could resist Dragon Sprouts with Dragonstone? Indeed!

INGREDIENTS

255g Dragon (kale) sprouts, trimmed
2 tblsp cold-pressed rapeseed oil
4 red chillies, seeded and thinly sliced
1 tsp white wine vinegar
2 cloves garlic sliced
2 tblsp soy sauce
½ tsp honey

METHOD

1   Heat the oil in a large frying pan, add the chillies and allow to cook, stirring for a few minutes.
2   Carefully add the vinegar and immediately throw in the sprouts and garlic. Stir-fry for a few minutes and then add the soy and honey. Check seasoning and serve.

Delicious on its own or with a pork dish.

BLANCHED CURLY KALE WITH DULSE

You can use any variety for this recipe but the more colourful ones do look good. Having said that, the brilliant green of Curly kale always looks good anyway! This recipe has a Japanesey feel to it and I have added some dulse flakes, which is optional, but gives a lovely mariney flavour. If you like a lot of heat, add chilli flakes instead.

INGREDIENTS

200g Curly kale fronds, shredded to "bite" size
Clove of garlic crushed
½ tsp peeled finely chopped root ginger
½ tsp dulse flakes
1 tblsp soy sauce
1 tblsp rice or cider vinegar
3 tblsp walnut oil
Hebridean seaweed salt

METHOD

1   Bring a pan of salted water to the boil and throw in the kale. Blanche for about 3 minutes and then drain and refresh in cold water to arrest the cooking.
2   When cold, drain and squeeze out the water and pat dry on a kitchen towel or paper.
3   Whisk together the remaining ingredients and leave for at least 30 minutes or until needed, and then mix with the kale in a bowl and serve.

BRAISED KALE WITH POLENTA

I love the colours in this simple dish and it's a great accompaniment for rich meat dishes or as a base for a vegetarian mushroom stew.

INGREDIENTS

500ml water
1 tsp Hebridean salt
100g polenta
A couple of handfuls of the base kale (Page 15)
2 cloves chopped garlic
1 tblsp olive oil
100g grated cheese

METHOD

1   Bring the pan of water to a rolling boil add the salt and pour in the polenta in a steady stream, whisking all the time. Once the polenta is all in, keep whisking and as it thickens lower the heat as it will splutter and spit! Hot polenta burns! Using a wooden spoon, stir the mixture for a few minutes.
2   Stir in the chopped, braised kale, the garlic the oil and grated cheese, pour onto a wooden board. You can use the polenta straight away or you can allow it to cool and cut into shapes which you can fry when needed.

KALE WITH SAUSAGES AND POTATO

Use your favourite sausage for this; it doesn't need to be anything fancy just a good pork sausage. You can also add some spice like cumin or paprika, just after the garlic stage. Only peel the potatoes if the skins are particularly blemished or hard. Most of the nutrients are just under the skin which you lose if you peel it.

INGREDIENTS

6 sausages
300g kale
1 tblsp rapeseed oil
1 onion peeled and chopped
2 cloves garlic crushed
500g potatoes cut in a chunky dice
100ml water
Hebridean sea salt
Coarsely ground black pepper

METHOD

1   Cook the sausages in the oven and cut into small chunks.
2   Separate the kale from the stalks and chop the stalks quite finely, and shred the leaves.
3   Take a frying pan and add the oil and sweat the onion with the kale stalks for a few minutes. Stir in the diced potatoes, and colour lightly. Add garlic , the salt and the shredded kale, stirring to coat.
4   Lower the heat and add the water and cover. Cook for about 10 minutes.
5   Remove the lid, raise the heat and add the sausages. The water will all evaporate; mix through thoroughly and check seasoning.

BRAISED PHEASANT BREAST WITH KALE AND PUY LENTILS

Kale is really good with big flavours and provides colour in what might otherwise be a dull-looking dish.

INGREDIENTS

200g puy lentils
2 tsp vegetable oil
4 pheasant breasts
2 tsp butter
1 onion peeled and finely chopped
2 cloves garlic peeled and crushed
2 sticks celery, cut to a small dice
2 medium carrots, cut to a small dice
200g kale roughly chopped
½ tsp Hebridean salt
Freshly ground black pepper

METHOD

1   Rinse the lentils in cold water and then place in a pan and cover with water bring to the boil and simmer for 10 minutes, drain and set aside.

2   Take a liddable pan and set it over a medium heat and add the oil. Dry the pheasant breasts on kitchen paper and brown on both sides, raising the heat as needed; remove and set aside.

3   Lower the heat, add the butter and the chopped onion, sweat gently to colour a little and then stir in the garlic, celery and carrots, add the lentils and water, enough to cover. Place the pheasant on top and cover. Cook gently until the water almost evaporates.

4   Take out the pheasant; stir in the kale to wilt, and cook for a few minutes. Season with a little salt and pepper. Serve with the pheasant on top.

SPICED KALE WITH COCONUT MILK AND SMOKED HAKE

The smokeyness of the fish goes well with the coconut milk and the colours are great too. Try using some Hebridean smoked salt to enhance the smoke, or even the seaweed-flavoured one.

INGREDIENTS

200g kale
4 cloves garlic peeled
2 whole red chillies seeded
2 tsp ground cumin
1 tsp ground coriander
½ tsp turmeric

2 tblsp vegetable oil
1 tsp whole cumin seeds
4 fillets of smoked hake
1 tsp Hebridean sea salt
4 tblsp coconut milk

METHOD

1   Trim the kale and remove the tough stalk ends and cut into roughly 3cm pieces.
2   Blitz the garlic and chilli together with enough water to form a light paste.
3   Pour into a bowl and add the three ground spices.
4   Heat a large pan with the oil and stir in the cumin seeds, stir gently until they sizzle. Turn the heat down and add the spice mix and fry for a few minutes.
5   Add the kale and stir to really mix through; add a little water. Push the fish fillets carefully into the mixture. Cover and cook gently for 10 minutes.
6   Remove the lid; add the coconut milk and raise the temperature. Cook until the mixture just coats the kale.

The mixture goes well with a curried lamb dish or other vegetable dishes, without the fish.

KALE AND CRIFFEL FLAN WITH CARDAMOM

Kale goes well with many other vegetables but this idea, borrowed from Tamasin Day Lewis's "Art of the Tart", creates a delicious tart, using a superb Scottish cheese from Dumfriesshire.

INGREDIENTS

Shortcrust pastry
2 bulbs of fennel
2 tblsp cold-pressed rapeseed oil
2 tblsp wine vinegar
½ tsp ground cardamom
4 tblsp cooked kale from the base recipe
1 tblsp crème fraiche
4 tblsp double cream
1 egg and 1 egg yolk
100ml milk
100g Criffel cheese
1 tsp Hebridean salt

METHOD

1   Roll out the pastry, line a 22cm flan case and bake blind in an oven 190C, gas mark 5. Leave the oven on.
2   Slice the fennel thinly and cook gently in a pan with the oil, vinegar and cardamom until soft.
3   Line the base of the flan case with the fennel, then cover with the shredded kale, followed by slices of the Criffel.
4   Whisk together the crème fraiche, cream, eggs and milk and add the salt.
5   Pour over the flan and bake in the oven for 25 minutes.

SALAD WITH WALNUTS, RADISH AND CROWDIE

Crowdie is a simple cream cheese and its delicate flavour and texture are a perfect foil for the strong flavours of the kale, radish and walnuts. I like to dress this with rapeseed oil and red wine vinegar but a lemon and walnut oil dressing would give a richer counterpoint to the salad.

INGREDIENTS

A mix of kales is good in this. I use Red Russian or Ragged Jack, and Curly for colour; a couple of good handfuls.
6 radishes
100g walnuts
6 tsp crowdie
3 tblsp cold-pressed rapeseed oil
1 tblsp red wine vinegar
Touch of mustard
1 tsp seaweed-flavoured Hebridean salt
Freshly ground black pepper

METHOD

1   Blanche and refresh the kale in boiling water, salted with Hebridean sea salt.
2   Dry carefully and place in a bowl.
3   Make the dressing by mixing together the oil, vinegar and mustard.
4   Mix the dressing lightly through the kale and place in a bowl. Sprinkle over the walnuts and sliced radish and dot with the crowdie.
5   Finish with a sprinkle of the seaweed-flavoured Hebridean salt and black pepper.

KALE AND MUSHROOM LASAGNE

Black kale is very good in this as it seems to go well with a white sauce and cheese. Satisfying enough for even the heartiest of meat eaters!

INGREDIENTS

Roughly 200g kale cooked in the base method (Page 15)
30g butter
400g sliced button mushrooms
¼ tsp mace
Lasagne sheets
20g grated Cheddar-type, hard cheese
Cold-pressed rapeseed oil
750ml whole milk
1 bay leaf
A few black peppercorns
50g butter
50g plain flour
1 tsp wholegrain mustard

METHOD

1   Preheat the oven to 180C, gas mark 4.
2   Fry the mushrooms in butter adding the mace, set aside.
3   Infuse the milk with the bay and peppercorns.
4   Make a white sauce with the butter, flour and hot milk, stir in the mustard.
5   Take a large ovenable dish @ 25cm sq or as close to this as you have.
6   Spread a bit of white sauce on the base and cover with lasagne sheets.
7   Spread over the cooked kale and a little more sauce, add another layer of lasagne.
8   Spread over the mushrooms and then another layer of lasagne.
9   Finish with sauce and grated cheese, swirl over a little oil and bake for 30 minutes.

RISOTTO OF KALE WITH ANSTER CHEESE AND RED WINE

I decided that red wine was the best for this as the kale obviously provides a strong flavour and I have used my local strong cheese but by all means use your own favourite to stir in at the end.

INGREDIENTS

2 litres chicken or vegetable stock
150g butter
1 onion peeled and chopped
5 stalks of Curly kale
2 cloves garlic crushed with tsp Hebridean sea salt
500g Arborio rice
375ml red wine
170g grated Anster cheese
Freshly ground black pepper
Splash rapeseed oil

METHOD

1   Bring the stock to a simmer and set aside.
2   Strip the kale leaves from the stalks and finely chop the stalks and shred the leaves.
3   Sweat the onions in a large pan with the butter and add the chopped stalks to soften.
4   Stir in the garlic and then add the rice and stir to mix through.
5   Start to add the stock, ladle by ladle, stirring all the time and adding more as the rice absorbs the liquid.
6   After about 3 ladles, add the shredded kale and keep stirring.
7   When the rice has just a bit of bite to it and the texture is creamy, check for seasoning and stir in the cheese.
8   Serve with a swirl of oil and a sprinkle of Hebridean salt.

SPICED BUBBLE AND SQUEAK CAKES WITH POACHED EGG AND SPINACH

The classic left-over mix, called Colcannon in Ireland; here I have mixed kale with potatoes and formed them into little cakes which, when served with spinach and a poached egg, becomes a splendid supper dish. This recipe uses raw kale but you can also just mix cooked kale with the potato.

INGREDIENTS

A little vegetable oil
1 onion peeled and chopped
8 leaves of Curly kale or equivalent of other kales,
    stalks removed and shredded separately
1 tsp cumin
½ tsp curry powder
Roughly 400g mashed potato
1 tsp Hebridean sea salt
Freshly ground black pepper

METHOD

1   Soften the onion in a pan with the oil and stir in the chopped kale stalks.
2   Stir in the spices and cook gently for a few minutes.
3   Stir in the shredded kale leaves, season and cover. Allow to cook gently for a few minutes; the steam from the kale will cook the mixture. Remove the lid and allow the moisture to evaporate. Cool.
4   Mix the potato with the kale and season with the salt and black pepper; form into small cakes or patties.
5   Fry in some butter and oil until lightly browned and hot through. Serve with some wilted spinach and a poached egg.

CALZONE

I could have called this a pasty but as the dough is yeast-based it's more of an Italian fold-over pizza, but you could use the mixture in a pasty recipe.

INGREDIENTS

500g strong white flour
Sachet of instant yeast
Warm water
Olive oil
1 tsp Hebridean salt
1 tsp butter
250g mushrooms sliced
2 shallots, peeled and chopped
300g kale stalks separated and shredded
150g crowdie

METHOD

1 Make a dough with the flour, yeast, water and oil and a little salt. Cover and leave to rise in a warm place.
2 Cook the mushrooms quickly in a little butter and oil and set aside.
3 Cook the shallots with the kale stalks in a little oil until soft, then stir in the chopped kale leaves. Cover and cook until soft. Season with Hebridean salt and black pepper; set aside to cool.
4 Turn the oven to 220C, gas mark 7.
5 Knock back the dough and roll out on a floured surface to a disc about 50cm in diameter. Spread the mushrooms over half the dough, leaving a border so that the other side can be folded over.
6 Cover the mushrooms with the kale mixture and top with the crowdie, just crumbled or spooned over. Moisten the edges and fold over the empty side and seal the edges. Allow to rest for about 20 minutes.
7 Have a baking sheet heating in the oven and slide the calzone on to it and bake for about 20 minutes. Serve drizzled with olive oil.

KALE AND CHICK PEA SALAD WITH SESAME SEEDS

This uses raw kale and again can be used with Ragged Jack, Curly or even Black kale but just remove the stalks. Marinating with garlic, ginger and red wine vinegar helps to soften the leaves without losing the lovely curly shape.

INGREDIENTS

6 heads of Curly kale or equivalent
1 tsp grated ginger root
2 cloves garlic crushed with some Hebridean salt (try the seaweed kind!)
1 tblsp red wine vinegar
400g tin of chick peas, drained
2 organic carrots grated
2 tblsp sesame oil
Lemon juice to taste
1 tblsp toasted sesame seeds

METHOD

1   Tear the kale into small pieces and discard the stalks.
2   Mix together the garlic, ginger and vinegar and rub gently into the kale leaves for a few minutes and leave for about 20 minutes.
3   Mix together with the carrot and chick peas; add the oil and lemon juice to taste.
4   Serve in a bowl with the sesame seeds sprinkled over.

PIROZHKI

Based on the Russian dish, these little pies are delicious fresh from the oven or as accompaniment to soups.

INGREDIENTS (for 12 pies)

200g plain white flour
200g stoneground brown bread flour
Sachet of yeast
2 tblsp cold-pressed rapeseed oil
1 tsp Hebridean sea salt
1 egg
About a tblsp of water
50g yogurt
Kale cooked as for Calzone (Page 43)
2 hard-boiled eggs
Egg wash

METHOD

1   Make a dough with the all the ingredients up to and including the yogurt adding more water if too dry and leave to rise.
2   Chop the hard-boiled eggs and add to the kale mixture.
3   Turn the oven to 180C, gas mark 4.
4   Knock the dough back and divide into 12, then roll each one out into 10cm rounds. Fill with a good blob of the kale and egg mixture. Moisten the edges and fold over and pinch the edges together.
5   Place upside down on a baking sheet with greaseproof paper. Brush with egg wash and leave to rise a little.
6   Bake for about 15-20 minutes until golden brown.

CREAMED KALE WITH PASTA

A simple sauce which can be used for any pasta or as a side dish.

INGREDIENTS

450g farfalle or whatever pasta you like
Kale cooked as in the base method
100ml double cream
100g grated cheddar
½ tsp paprika

METHOD

1   Cook the pasta as per packet but always keep a little of the cooking water back.
2   Blitz the kale in a food processor with the cream. Add the spice to form a smooth sauce; add a little water if necessary.
3   Mix with the cooked pasta. Serve with some grated cheese on top.

KALE AND APPLE SMOOTHIE

Kale in its raw state is of course very healthy but does have quite a strong flavour, so matching it with a sweet apple, and undercurrent of ginger, really helps to create a great smoothie. It is best served unstrained for all the goodness but for a smoother finish you may prefer to pour it through a sieve.

INGREDIENTS

2 good handfuls of kale, stalks removed
2 desert apples cored
2cm chunk of root ginger peeled
Juice of a lemon
Water or apple juice
100g cucumber

METHOD

1 Roughly chop up the ingredients.
2 Blitz the whole lot together until really smooth, adding liquid to get correct consistency.

KALE WITH CHORIZO AND GOATS CHEESE BAKE

I did this with bacon initially but the venison chorizo from Great Glen Game is great, but don't worry if you can't find it, 6 rashers of cooked bacon will do instead.

INGREDIENTS

1 basic mix of kale
Pack of Great Glen venison chorizo (75g)
6 eggs
250ml milk
100g hard goats' cheese grated
½ tsp Hebridean sea salt
Freshly ground black pepper

METHOD

1   Turn the oven on to 180C, gas mark 4.
2   Layer a gratin or a le creuset dish with the cooked, wilted kale.
3   Then place the slices of chorizo or bacon on top.
4   Mix the milk with the eggs and season and pour over the top.
5   Sprinkle liberally with the goats' cheese.
6   Bake in the oven until brown and lightly set.

BLACK RICE WITH CAVOLO NERO AND SESAME OIL

This dish looks very black! But the flavour of black rice is unique and partners the Black kale very well. I add a splash of sesame oil at the end but a good walnut oil also brings out the nuttiness of the rice.

INGREDIENTS

2 tsp butter
1 onion peeled and chopped
300g black rice
Can of chopped tomatoes
Litre of chicken or vegetable stock
1 bay leaf
400g Black kale (Cavolo Nero) cooked in the base method and
    finely chopped
2 tblsp grated hard cheddar
Sesame oil
½ tsp Hebridean sea salt
Freshly ground black pepper

METHOD

1   Gently sweat the onion in the butter for a few minutes to soften.
2   Stir in the rice and cook to heat through. Bring the stock to the boil and pour on. Add the tomatoes and bay leaf. Stir to combine.
3   Allow to simmer gently until the rice is cooked.
4   Stir in the Black kale and heat through.
5   Stir in the grated cheese and season with Hebridean salt and black pepper.

Serve with the drizzled sesame oil. Very good on its own or to accompany roasts.

KALE CRISPS

As with many ideas, this is simplicity itself but it is important to get a few things right otherwise you can end up with a soggy black mess. You can use any kale for this. I must thank Erin Spence from the wonderful Ardross Farm shop for this idea.

INGREDIENTS

Good bunch of kale, stalks removed
Cold-pressed rapeseed oil
Smoked Hebridean sea salt

METHOD

1   Heat the oven to 175C, gas mark 3.
2   Tear the kale into crisp-size pieces and wash and dry thoroughly. The drying is very important; there must be no water adhering.
3   Pour over a tablespoon of oil and gently massage the leaves with the oil, making sure they are well coated. If the oil doesn't completely coat the leaves, they can dry out and burn.
4   Spread thinly on a baking sheet and bake for 5-10 minutes in the oven.
5   Leave to rest for a few minutes before sprinkling over the smoked sea salt.

KALE PIZZA

You can use your favourite pizza dough for this but I tend to prefer an almost-white dough, with a little brown flour added.

INGREDIENTS

400g strong white flour
100g wholemeal bread flour
2 tsp dried yeast
½ tsp Hebridean sea salt
Cold-pressed rapeseed oil
About 320ml warm water
Butter
100g mushrooms sliced
1 large onion thinly sliced
3 cloves garlic thinly sliced
Large bunch Curly kale stalks and leaves separated and shredded
A few sundried tomatoes
100g grated hard cheddar

METHOD

1   Make a dough with the flours, a tablespoon of oil, yeast, salt and water. Leave to rise in a warm place.
2   Cook the mushrooms in a large frying pan with a little butter and set aside.
3   In the same pan, soften the onions with a little oil and then stir in the kale stalks. Cook gently for a few minutes to soften and then stir on the shredded kale and garlic. Cook gently for a few minutes.
4   Knock the dough back and split into two; roll out into two discs as thin as you can. Spread over the kale mix, sprinkling on the mushrooms, a few sundried tomatoes and cheese.
5   Splurge over some more oil; and bake for 10-15 minutes.

KALE QUINOA AND SWEET POTATO

A pretty dish as a vegetable or on its own. Good as a BBQ side dish.

INGREDIENTS

225g quinoa
Water
1 tsp Hebridean salt
Cold-pressed rapeseed oil
1 red onion sliced thinly
1 sweet potato cut in chunks
2 handfuls kale cooked in the base recipe

METHOD

1   Cook the quinoa in a pan of boiling water, salted with the Hebridean salt, for 15 minutes and drain.
2   In a frying pan, soften the red onion slices in the oil and set aside, then fry the sweet potato chunks to get a bit of colour. Once just cooked, stir in the chopped kale and quinoa to heat through, and season.
3   Serve with the red onion strewn over the top, a few chopped dried apricots look pretty too.

KALE BRUSCHETTA

A simple way to get your greens! But make sure the bread base is a good one, either a sourdough or a crusty ciabatta.

INGREDIENTS

8 slices of crusty bread, from a long round-style loaf
5 cloves garlic
A good handful of kale cooked in the base style
Cold-pressed rapeseed oil
1 tsp Hebridean sea salt
Shavings of a good hard goats' cheese, such as Bonnet

METHOD

1 Lightly toast the bread slices. Cut a clove of garlic in half and dip one half in the sea salt and rub over the toasted tops of the bread; brush with a little oil.
2 Chop the remaining garlic with a little Hebridean salt to create a paste and then chop the prepared kale with it; place in a bowl and mix with a little oil.
3 Spread over the toasts and cut shavings of goats' cheese over the top.

KILMANY KALE

Based on an old recipe from the village of Kilmany in Fife, where rabbits were plentiful. This needs some preparation ahead of time.

INGREDIENTS

2 tblsp virgin olive oil
Zest and juice of a lemon
4 cloves garlic crushed with a tsp of Hebridean sea salt
Freshly Ground black pepper
2 tblsp honey
2 tsp freshly chopped rosemary
2 tsp freshly chopped thyme
2 rabbits cut into 4 (legs and the saddle in two); use the front legs for another dish
Good bunch of Russian kale

METHOD

1   Mix the oil, lemon juice, zest, garlic and honey and set aside a tablespoon of the mixture.
2   Place the rabbit pieces in the main mix and add the herbs, and black pepper. Rub all over the rabbit and marinade for at least a couple of hours or overnight.
3   Grill the rabbit pieces for about 20 minutes and leave to rest.
4   Mix the kale leaves with the reserved oil and lemon juice thoroughly and then cook on the grill for a few minutes until crisp.

KALE WITH GINGER AND MUSTARD SEEDS

A simple way of cooking the kale as an accompanying vegetable for spicy foods.

INGREDIENTS

2 tsp mustard seeds
1 tblsp cold-pressed rapeseed oil
A good handful of Ragged Jack kale, roughly chopped
2cm piece of root ginger peeled and grated
½ tsp Hebridean sea salt
Sesame oil

METHOD

1   Take a dry pan and heat the mustard seeds until they begin to pop.
2   Add the oil and the kale and mix through to wilt.
3   Stir in the ginger and salt.
4   Cook gently until soft, serve with sesame oil swirled over.

BIOGRAPHIES

CAROLINE TROTTER is a freelance photographer and works across a wide variety of subjects. Weddings are her main area of work but she also does portraits, both human and animal – horses, dogs etc. Caroline covers events for associations such as Fife Chamber of Commerce and provides business portraits for websites and marketing purposes. She also runs photography courses from home.

www.carolinetrotter.co.uk

CHRISTOPHER TROTTER is Fife's Food Ambassador, an honorary title bestowed on him for his work promoting food from Fife. He is also a freelance chef, cookery writer and food commentator, appearing on programmes such as BBC Radio Scotland's *Kitchen Café* and *Kitchen Garden*. He is a committee member of The Guild Of Food Writers and is a sought after speaker at events and after dinner. As a consultant he has worked with agencies as diverse as Argyll and the Island's Enterprise and The National Trust for Scotland. Christopher also provides cookery classes and food tours and he is passionate about fresh produce in its season.

www.fifefoodambassador.co.uk

They have two children, four hens (currently), two dogs and a mac cat. And live in rural Fife.

ACKNOWLEDGEMENTS AND THANKS

This is my third little vegetable book and I will continue the series until I run out of steam and/or vegetables! Thanks therefore goes to everyone who has bought a copy of "Beetroot" and "Courgette" and to those who continue to do so. And on the book selling front continued thanks to Waterstones in St Andrews and in particular Stuart Paterson and Julie Thow.

Bruce Bennett at Pillars of Hercules in Falkland in Fife made me realise that there was more than just one kale! And has provided some of the kale for the pics.

Thanks to my beautiful wife Caroline who always makes my simple food look great!

To Carolyn Scott for digging out recipes almost as old as her!

And to the many cheffy /cooking friends who through conversations have contributed to this book, in particular David Naylor, Alison Sykora, Graeme Pallister and Tim Dover, and all my colleagues on the committee of the Guild of Food Writers – a truly inspiring bunch!

Also to my brother Graeme who has waded through and edited my tortured Grammer . . .

I am often asked who my "foodie" heroes are so once again:
Thanks to Myrtle Allen Sybil Kapoor Nigel Slater, Yotam Ottolenghi, Jane Baxter Rowley Leigh, Roger Verge, Michel Guerard, and many more.

HEBRIDEAN SEA SALT

Sea Salt Flakes harvested from the shores of the remote Scottish Hebridean Isle of Lewis.

SIMPLY FROM THE SEA

Hebridean Sea Salt is Scotland's first gourmet salt producer. Nestled on the banks of Loch Erisort, on the Isle of Lewis in the Outer Hebrides, we harvest sea water from some of the most unspoilt coastline in the world. The waters around the Hebrides are crystal clear and have been given a grade A certification, which creates pure white crunchy sea salt flakes that melt in the mouth.

PURE ORIGINAL SEA SALT

Our most popular variety, the Pure Original sea salt was the first to be launched by the company in 2012. With over 60 naturally occurring minerals such as essentials like Potassium, Zinc, Calcium & Magnesium it is a wonderful alternative to table salts. It is best added to meals and cooking by hand, 'a pinch' is just enough to enhance the natural flavours of your food.

PEAT SMOKED SEA SALT

Delicately cold smoked with a mixture of oak and peat cut from the surrounding moor, our peat smoked variety adds an extra depth of flavour to any meal. Peat is very much a part of the Hebridean landscape, the unmistakeable smell fills the air daily. Used as a rub for meats, or on a simple salad, once you've started using our Peat Smoked salt it will become a regular at every mealtime.

SEAWEED INFUSED SEA SALT

Our Pure Original sea salt and locally harvested seaweed make for the perfect seasoning combination. With its rich and distinctive flavour seaweed is packed full of essential nutrients. The people of the Hebrides have been harvesting seaweed to supplement their diets for hundreds of years. Use our Seaweed Infused sea salt to season fish, giving it an added taste of the sea or in sushi or sauces. Seaweed also has a naturally salty flavour, so this is a useful way to cut down on your salt in-take if you need to.

AN AWARD WINNING RANGE

Hebridean Sea Salt is regularly awarded Great Taste stars at the annual Guild of Fine Food's 'Oscars' of the food world. We hope you will also find Hebridean Sea Salt a winning combination when teamed with your cooking.

NOTES

NOTES

NOTES

NOTES